Approaches to Learning

The HighScope Preschool Curriculum

Approaches to Learning

Ann S. Epstein, PhD

HIGHSCOPE PRESS ®

Ypsilanti, Michigan

Published by
HighScope® Press

A division of the
HighScope Educational Research Foundation
600 North River Street
Ypsilanti, Michigan 48198-2898
734.485.2000, FAX 734.485.0704
Orders: 800.40.PRESS; Fax: 800.442.4FAX; www.highscope.org
E-mail: *press@highscope.org*

Editor: Marcella Fecteau Weiner
Cover design, text design: Judy Seling, Seling Design LLC
Production: Judy Seling, Seling Design LLC; Kazuko Sacks, Profit Makers LLC
Photography:
Jan Levanger Dowling & Terri C. Mitchell — 25
Bob Foran — 3, 4, 11, 13, 14 (KDI 3), 19, 31, 50, 53, 57 (bottom), 59 (top), back cover (bottom left)
Gregory Fox — Front cover, 6, 14 (KDI 1, KDI 2), 15, 21, 23, 26, 29, 30, 33, 37, 39, 47, 49, 56, 59 (bottom), 60, 63, 64, 66, back cover (right)
Pat Thompson — 24, 57
HighScope Staff — All other photos

Library of Congress Cataloging-in-Publication Data
Epstein, Ann S.
  Approaches to learning / Ann S. Epstein.
    p. cm. -- (The Highscope preschool curriculum)
  ISBN 978-1-57379-651-4 (soft cover : alk. paper) 1. Education, Preschool--Curricula. 2. Education, Preschool--Activity programs. I. Title.
  LB1140.4.E67 2012
  372.21--dc23
                                        2012003665
Printed in the United States of America
10 9 8 7 6 5 4 3 2

Contents

Acknowledgments

Many people contributed their knowledge and skills to the publication of *Approaches to Learning*. I want to thank the Early Childhood staff as well as other HighScope staff members who collaborated on creating the key developmental indicators (KDIs) in this content area: Beth Marshall, Sue Gainsley, Shannon Lockhart, Polly Neill, Kay Rush, Julie Hoelscher, and Emily Thompson. Among this group of colleagues, those who devoted special attention to reviewing the manuscript for this book were Beth Marshall and Julie Hoelscher. Mary Hohmann, whose expertise informs many other books about the HighScope Curriculum, also provided detailed feedback.

The developmental scaffolding charts in this volume — describing what children might do and say and how adults can support and gently extend their learning at different developmental levels — are invaluable contributions to the curriculum. I am grateful to Beth Marshall and Sue Gainsley for the extraordinary working relationship we forged in creating these charts. By bringing our unique experiences to this challenging process, we integrated knowledge about child development and effective classroom practices from the perspectives of research, teaching, training, and policy.

Thanks are also due to Nancy Brickman, who directed the editing and production of the book. I extend particular appreciation to Marcella Fecteau Weiner, who edited the volume, and Katie Bruckner, who assisted with all aspects of the publication process. I also want to acknowledge the following individuals for contributing to the book's visual appeal and reader friendliness: photographers Bob Foran and Gregory Fox and graphic artists Judy Seling (book design) and Kazuko Sacks (book production).

Finally, I extend sincerest thanks to all the teachers, trainers, children, and families whose participation in HighScope and other early childhood programs has contributed to the creation and authenticity of the HighScope Preschool Curriculum over the decades. I hope this book continues to support the development of their approaches to learning for many years to come.

CHAPTER 1

The Importance of
Approaches to Learning

What Is Approaches to Learning?

Approaches to learning describes how young children go about acquiring new knowledge and mastering skills. Adults are always learning too, for example, when we move to a new city and map our route to work, buy an electronic gadget and teach ourselves to operate it, or meet new people and tentatively explore becoming friends. Our approach to learning about objects, events, and people is one of the characteristics that defines who we are and how we relate to the world.

Approaches to learning is the foundation that affects how children learn in *every* content area. It encompasses children's engagement, motivation, and participation in the classroom. Researcher Ross Thompson (2002) says that when young children are curious, interested, and confident about discovering the answers to their questions, they are best able to benefit from learning opportunities. This conclusion is supported by the work of many others. For example, studies based on teacher and parent ratings find approaches to learning at school entry predicts reading and mathematics achievement through the primary grades (Alexander, Entwistle, & Dauber, 1993; Duncan, Claessens, & Engle, 2005; Li-Grining, Maldonado-Carreño, Votruba-Drzal, & Haas, 2010).

Young children approach learning in different ways, each bringing a unique set of attitudes, habits, and preferences to their interactions and explorations. They differ on whether they approach life with enthusiasm or reserve, are flummoxed or challenged by problems, plan ahead or react to circumstances, and are open or resistant to new experiences and ideas. Adults must consider these individual characteristics, together with general developmental trends, as they support learning in each child and the class as a whole.

Approaches to Learning in Action

At work time in the house area, Claire is disappointed when she cannot find baby clothes to dress her doll. Her teacher Becky says the clothes are in the wash and asks what else Claire could use. "I can make clothes!" Claire exclaims with enthusiasm. "I'll get paper." She and Becky wrap, cut, and tape paper around the doll. Two more children join them. Claire spends a lot of time cutting small pieces of paper and taping them on the doll's feet for "socks."

❖

At work time in the block area, Matthew sees that the pen he is making for Valentine, the classroom guinea pig, has an opening where the pet can escape. He gets a large block to cover the hole.

❖

At cleanup time in the art area, Curtis looks at the tiny cut-up pieces of Styrofoam on the floor. His teacher Shannon wonders how he will get them up. Curtis says, "I can use the broom and dustpan" and then proceeds to the kitchen area to get them. When he finishes sweeping up the Styrofoam, he empties the pieces into the trash.

❖

At recall time, Shamar describes what he did in the block area at work time: "I put out the fire all by myself. I got the hose and sprayed the chemicals until the fire stopped."

Preschool programs are often children's first learning experiences outside their homes. How children approach learning in these early years, thus, can determine their attitudes toward education when they enter school, and indeed, for the rest of their lives. By understanding how to support this area of early development, adults can foster children with Claire's resourcefulness, Matthew's foresight, Curtis's persistence, and Shamar's initiative, as illustrated by the anecdotes in "Approaches to Learning in Action" on the facing page.

Components of Approaches to Learning

Although a child's approach to learning is central to every aspect of education, this area of development is not easy to define and measure. The National Education Goals Panel (Kagan, Moore, & Bredekamp, 1995) says approaches to learning include curiosity, creativity, confidence, independence, initiative, and persistence. This list covers what psychologists call *dispositions,* defined by early childhood educators Lilian Katz and Diane McClellan (1997) as "enduring habits of mind and characteristic ways of responding to experiences" (p. 6). Dispositions include *styles of learning* and attitudes toward education. Such traits are especially hard to measure in young children who lack the words to describe their work style or educational beliefs.

However, adults can more readily observe some of these behaviors or skills. For example, we can see whether children take the initiative to explore materials and ideas, or independently solve problems, as they carry out their intentions. Adults can also see and measure engagement, or concentration and persistence with a task. This was the case in a Seattle classroom, where a teacher participating in

"Approaches to learning describes not the *what* but the *how* of learning.... Today young children's interest, engagement, persistence, and motivation are being placed at risk [due to] the challenges of poverty, violence, and instability within families and communities; trends in early childhood curriculum, teaching, and assessment practices; and the inadequate supply of evidence-based professional development. The risks are many but so are the remedies. Action is needed to remove barriers and to direct greater attention to approaches to learning."

— Hyson (2008, pp. 4, 12)

Children approach learning in different ways. Some are more reserved, while other children approach new experiences with lots of enthusiasm.

Styles of Learning

Psychologists and educators use the term *styles of learning* to describe how people go about acquiring knowledge and skills, solving problems, and generally dealing with the information and experiences the world presents. Individual differences in styles of learning appear early in childhood and persist into adulthood. These differences vary along several dimensions, including sensory mode, pace or timing, and social context.

Some children, for example, are visually oriented. They learn primarily through sight, observing objects, examining patterns and relationships, and watching the behavior of others. Others may be better at processing information orally and respond well to verbal descriptions and directions. Still another set of individuals needs to handle and manipulate objects to fully grasp how things work. While using this tactile mode is characteristic of young children in general, for some people a preference for learning through touching and doing persists into adulthood.

There are also individual differences with regard to the pace of learning. Some children do well with a faster pace and can shift rapidly from one activity or experience to another. As adults, they may succeed at multitasking or be more open to change. Other children are slower and more deliberate in the way they process information. They focus on one thing at a time and transition gradually between activities or ideas.

Finally, children and adults also differ in whether they learn best by working on their own or interacting with others. Some thrive on independent pursuits, quietly and methodically investigating things or practicing skills. Others learn well in a group context. They find that the give and take of social exchange helps them consider new ideas and master new skills.

Everyone uses virtually every style of learning at some point in their ongoing education, depending on the subject matter or the situation in which they find themselves. However, a preference for certain modes predominates in their approach to learning. And while some of these differences are due to innate temperamental differences — the dispositions or tendencies we are born with — our environment and educational experiences also play a major role in shaping the ways we can and do learn.

By providing young children with a variety of options and opportunities, the HighScope Preschool Curriculum respects individual differences while also allowing children to discover and develop competence in other modes of learning. And because formal schooling (and the subjects children must master) often requires them to learn in certain ways, helping them develop positive and adaptive approaches to learning prepares them for future success.

*Some children learn best by **watching** others — watching the teacher and other children use the straws and golf balls before trying it themselves. Other children learn by **doing** right off the bat — using the straws and golf balls in their own way.*

HighScope training began to provide more choices in the materials and activities she offered and noted in her journal, "Children are staying with a task much longer because it is more open ended, and matches their interests and ability levels."

Approaches to learning also involves being able to break down a task into its components, organize a plan of work, and reflect on the success of one's endeavors. In these respects, a child's approach to learning affects performance in other content areas. For example, it can determine whether the child asks a teacher for help writing a letter of the alphabet versus finding one to copy, or builds a small tower alone versus collaborating with others to construct a bigger or more complex one.

Influences on Approaches to Learning

A child's approach to learning is in part shaped by temperament, including the child's level of inhibition and strength of emotional reactions (Chess & Alexander, 1996). Babies are born with innate temperamental differences that persist into adulthood. However, the Collaborative for the Advancement of Social and Emotional Learning (Elias et al., 1997) says that the environment also plays a significant role in determining how these biological traits are expressed. For example, persistence lets a child solve problems, but if it turns into stubbornness, it may interfere with the ability to meet challenges and form satisfying social relationships. By offering realistic choices and being alert to signs of frustration, adults make it possible for the child to channel perseverance positively and productively rather than negatively persisting with an idea or behavior that is not productive. Thus, the responsiveness of the environment can help shape the way

children use the traits they are born with to deal with materials, people, and events in their world.

The National Education Goals Panel emphasizes that school readiness is enhanced when young children are encouraged to explore, ask questions, and use their imaginations. These early experiences predispose them to take reasonable risks. HighScope uses the term *initiative* to describe children's desire and ability to begin and follow through on tasks. Children intentionally decide what, how, and with whom to engage. They do so with a specific goal or plan in mind. The child's goal may be simple (get the ball) or complex (write my name with a stick in the sand). By encouraging young children to follow their own interests, the HighScope Preschool Curriculum supports the development of initiative and intentionality. Children's play is purposeful and confident, as noted by this teacher from Phoenix, Arizona, after she began to implement the HighScope Preschool Curriculum in her classroom: "Children are more actively involved, self-assertive, independent, and have more opportunities to develop their environment. They feel ownership of the classroom, show pride in their accomplishments, and can take care of their own needs. Their satisfied attitude and confidence just shine through!"

While many early childhood programs allow children to make choices, HighScope preschools incorporate the **plan-do-review process,** which encourages children to engage in *planning.* During **planning time** (plan), children state, in gestures or words, a plan of action. At **work time** (do), children carry out their initial plans and other self-initiated activities, working and playing alone or with others while adults interact with children to support and gently extend their activities. At the end of work time is **recall time** (review), at which time children reflect on, share, and discuss their work-time experiences. (For more detailed information about

During planning time, this child uses a small car to drive to the area she plans to work in during work time on the classroom "roadmap." As she plans, she is thinking about and expressing an intention of what she is going to do.

What the Research Says

"Research [on approaches to learning] is clear on at least five points:

1. Children begin to develop these characteristics and behaviors at an early age.

2. Even in the early years, children differ in their approaches to learning.

3. These differences influence children's school readiness and school success.

4. Children's experiences at home and in early childhood programs can strengthen or undermine their positive approaches to learning.

5. Early childhood programs can implement specific strategies that will promote positive approaches to learning in areas such as strengthening relationships with children, working together with families, designing supportive classroom environments, and selecting effective curriculum and teaching methods."

— Hyson (2008, p. 3)

plan-do-review, see chapter 8 in *The HighScope Preschool Curriculum*, Epstein & Hohmann, 2012.)

The difference between simply making a choice (red or blue beads?) and making a plan (what will I do at work time?) — the first component in the plan-do-review process — is that planning involves thinking about and expressing an intention. Preschoolers' plans reflect the activities they want to initiate and pursue, including where they want to work and the materials (dress-up clothes) or ideas (playing "fireman") they want to engage with. Their plans may also include the people they intend to work with ("Jeremy and I are going to feed Squiggy [the hamster] and clean out his cage"). Young children continue to express their intentions throughout the day, whether they are using their imaginations ("Wake up when the good witch says 'pop'"), solving problems ("Tim, hold this down so I can glue it"), or voicing desires

and frustration ("I want to use the computer but Schuyler got there first!").

Approaches to learning thus cut across all domains of development. They reflect what we think of as children's personalities, or emotional dispositions. Because so much early learning occurs in social settings, children's social dispositions can also affect their exposure and openness to new information. Finally, whether children perceive learning and problem solving as positive challenges, insurmountable barriers, or even threats directly affects their ability to benefit from their educational experiences. How young children approach learning carries long past their entry into formal schooling. In fact, it will likely determine their educational careers and influence their attitude toward mastering new knowledge and skills throughout their adult lives. For these reasons, it is important to provide young children with experiences that develop their initiative and the skills to solve problems with confidence, flexibility, and persistence.

About This Book

In the HighScope Preschool Curriculum, the content of children's learning is organized into eight areas: A. Approaches to Learning; B. Social and Emotional Development; C. Physical Development and Health; D. Language, Literacy, and Communication; E. Mathematics; F. Creative Arts; G. Science and Technology; and H. Social Studies. Within each content area, HighScope identifies **key developmental indicators (KDIs)** that are the building blocks of young children's thinking and reasoning.

The term *key developmental indicators* encapsulates HighScope's approach to early education. The word *key* refers to the fact that these are the meaningful ideas children should learn and experience. The second part of the term — *developmental* — conveys the idea that learning is gradual and cumulative. Learning follows a sequence, generally moving from simple to more complex knowledge and skills. Finally, we chose the term *indicators* to emphasize that educators need evidence that children are developing the knowledge, skills, and understanding considered important for school and life readiness. To plan appropriately for students and to evaluate program effectiveness, we need observable indicators of our impact on children.

This book is designed to help you as you guide and support young children's learning in the Approaches to Learning content area in the HighScope Curriculum. This chapter provided insights from research literature on how children approach learning and summarized basic principles of how children acquire knowledge and skills. Chapter 2 describes general teaching strategies for Approaches to Learning and provides an overview of the KDIs for this content area.

Chapters 3–8, respectively, provide teaching strategies for each of the six KDIs in Approaches to Learning:

1. **Initiative:** Children demonstrate initiative as they explore their world.

2. **Planning:** Children make plans and follow through on their intentions.

3. **Engagement:** Children focus on activities that interest them.

4. **Problem solving:** Children solve problems encountered in play.

5. **Use of resources:** Children gather information and formulate ideas about their world.

6. **Reflection:** Children reflect on their experiences.

At the end of each of these chapters is a chart showing ideas for scaffolding learning for that KDI. The chart will help you recognize the specific abilities that are developing at earlier, middle, and later stages of development and gives corresponding teaching strategies that you can use to support and gently extend children's learning at each stage.

HighScope Preschool Curriculum Content
Key Developmental Indicators

A. Approaches to Learning

1. **Initiative:** Children demonstrate initiative as they explore their world.

2. **Planning:** Children make plans and follow through on their intentions.

3. **Engagement:** Children focus on activities that interest them.

4. **Problem solving:** Children solve problems encountered in play.

5. **Use of resources:** Children gather information and formulate ideas about their world.

6. **Reflection:** Children reflect on their experiences.

B. Social and Emotional Development

7. **Self-identity:** Children have a positive self-identity.

8. **Sense of competence:** Children feel they are competent.

9. **Emotions:** Children recognize, label, and regulate their feelings.

10. **Empathy:** Children demonstrate empathy toward others.

11. **Community:** Children participate in the community of the classroom.

12. **Building relationships:** Children build relationships with other children and adults.

13. **Cooperative play:** Children engage in cooperative play.

14. **Moral development:** Children develop an internal sense of right and wrong.

15. **Conflict resolution:** Children resolve social conflicts.

C. Physical Development and Health

16. **Gross-motor skills:** Children demonstrate strength, flexibility, balance, and timing in using their large muscles.

17. **Fine-motor skills:** Children demonstrate dexterity and hand-eye coordination in using their small muscles.

18. **Body awareness:** Children know about their bodies and how to navigate them in space.

19. **Personal care:** Children carry out personal care routines on their own.

20. **Healthy behavior:** Children engage in healthy practices.

D. Language, Literacy, and Communication[1]

21. **Comprehension:** Children understand language.

22. **Speaking:** Children express themselves using language.

23. **Vocabulary:** Children understand and use a variety of words and phrases.

24. **Phonological awareness:** Children identify distinct sounds in spoken language.

25. **Alphabetic knowledge:** Children identify letter names and their sounds.

26. **Reading:** Children read for pleasure and information.

27. **Concepts about print:** Children demonstrate knowledge about environmental print.

28. **Book knowledge:** Children demonstrate knowledge about books.

29. **Writing:** Children write for many different purposes.

30. **English language learning:** (If applicable) Children use English and their home language(s) (including sign language).

---

[1]Language, Literacy, and Communication KDIs 21–29 may be used for the child's home language(s) as well as English. KDI 30 refers specifically to English language learning.

E. Mathematics

31. **Number words and symbols:** Children recognize and use number words and symbols.

32. **Counting:** Children count things.

33. **Part-whole relationships:** Children combine and separate quantities of objects.

34. **Shapes:** Children identify, name, and describe shapes.

35. **Spatial awareness:** Children recognize spatial relationships among people and objects.

36. **Measuring:** Children measure to describe, compare, and order things.

37. **Unit:** Children understand and use the concept of unit.

38. **Patterns:** Children identify, describe, copy, complete, and create patterns.

39. **Data analysis:** Children use information about quantity to draw conclusions, make decisions, and solve problems.

F. Creative Arts

40. **Art:** Children express and represent what they observe, think, imagine, and feel through two- and three-dimensional art.

41. **Music:** Children express and represent what they observe, think, imagine, and feel through music.

42. **Movement:** Children express and represent what they observe, think, imagine, and feel through movement.

43. **Pretend play:** Children express and represent what they observe, think, imagine, and feel through pretend play.

44. **Appreciating the arts:** Children appreciate the creative arts.

G. Science and Technology

45. **Observing:** Children observe the materials and processes in their environment.

46. **Classifying:** Children classify materials, actions, people, and events.

47. **Experimenting:** Children experiment to test their ideas.

48. **Predicting:** Children predict what they expect will happen.

49. **Drawing conclusions:** Children draw conclusions based on their experiences and observations.

50. **Communicating ideas:** Children communicate their ideas about the characteristics of things and how they work.

51. **Natural and physical world:** Children gather knowledge about the natural and physical world.

52. **Tools and technology:** Children explore and use tools and technology.

H. Social Studies

53. **Diversity:** Children understand that people have diverse characteristics, interests, and abilities.

54. **Community roles:** Children recognize that people have different roles and functions in the community.

55. **Decision making:** Children participate in making classroom decisions.

56. **Geography:** Children recognize and interpret features and locations in their environment.

57. **History:** Children understand past, present, and future.

58. **Ecology:** Children understand the importance of taking care of their environment.

CHAPTER 2

General Teaching Strategies
for Approaches to Learning

Adults can help young children develop positive approaches to learning by creating a learning environment that supports their emerging sense of themselves as doers and thinkers. Children will enjoy and gain something meaningful from their endeavors when adults use the following general strategies to encourage a variety of learning styles in individuals and the class as a whole.

General Teaching Strategies

Establish a physical environment that is rich in options to explore materials, actions, ideas, and relationships

Young children enter preschool primed for new experiences. They bring to this exciting but unknown environment a shared curiosity and motivation to learn, along with unique dispositions about how to approach the process of discovery. As detailed in chapter 6 in *The HighScope Preschool Curriculum* (Epstein & Hohmann, 2012), a classroom that is arranged and equipped for active learning allows children to do things on their own and in their own way. Being able to choose among many options to find those that match their interests and personalities lets children gain confidence in their ability to explore, answer their own questions, form meaningful relationships, and draw conclusions about how the world and its inhabitants work, as shown in the following anecdote:

After they return from summer vacation, Neil and Josh play camping out several times a week. Their teacher adds blankets to the house area that they drape over chairs for tents. They use blocks for flashlights and a baby bottle as a canteen. Neil's father brings in an extra sleeping bag, and several children invent a guessing game where they hide things inside it.

Create a daily routine that allows children to express a variety of learning styles and preferences

Predictable routines establish a safe setting within which young children can approach the job of learning in whatever ways feel comfortable for them. A combination of child- and adult-initiated activities, during individual and group times of the day, provides a range of experiences to suit children's needs, interests, and preferred modes of engaging with materials, ideas, actions, and people.

In HighScope preschool programs, teachers follow a daily routine, which includes the following activities:

- Greeting time
- Planning time
- Work time
- Cleanup time
- Recall time
- Large-group time
- Eating and resting times
- Small-group time
- Outside time
- Transition times (including arrival and departure)

Planning time, work time, cleanup time, and recall time always occur in the same order (one right after the other). The order of the other activities, however, may vary, depending on a program's hours. For example, for half-day programs, each activity happens once, while in full-day programs, one or more activities may be repeated. In addition, a number of these activities, such as planning time, work time, and recall time, are child initiated, whereas other activities, such as small- and large-group times, are adult initiated.

> "It is fundamentally misleading to think about a single mind, a single intelligence, a single problem-solving capacity."
>
> — Gardner (1983/2003, p. 8)

A consistent yet flexible daily routine ensures that children's individual approaches to learning will be acknowledged and respected, as shown in this anecdote:

At work time, Jerry paints alone at the easel, then asks the teacher to read him a book. During small-group time, he adds a sticker to Matt's row and tells him, "Now yours is as long as mine." They take turns adding stickers to each other's papers. Jerry leads the class in a movement at large-group time; he taps his nose to the beat and the other children copy his action. At outside time, when Matt asks Jerry if he wants to go on the climber with him, Jerry shakes his head no. He rides a bicycle until it is time to go home.

Give children time to approach learning in their own way

Many adults live with the constant pressure of multiple demands and tight schedules. Without realizing it, we inadvertently impose these constraints on children. Yet preschoolers need time

Children are more likely to problem-solve if adults give them time to figure out for themselves how to find a solution.

Approaches to Learning in Action

KDI 1. Initiative

KDI 2. Planning

KDI 3. Engagement

KDI 4. *Problem solving*

KDI 5. *Use of resources*

KDI 6. *Reflection*

and psychological space to attempt new things, make a plan, figure out how to solve a problem, practice a new skill, and think about the meaning of what they just saw or heard. It is therefore important for adults to be patient as children approach experiences in their own way. When adults step in too quickly to suggest a plan, offer a solution, or do something for the child, they deprive the child of an opportunity to discover and create things for him or herself. Although adults may satisfy their own internal pressure, children may become anxious, resentful, or disinterested. They also learn to rely on the adult for ideas. Children are more apt to take the initiative, solve problems, and flourish as planners and thinkers when they can take their time approaching the many opportunities for learning in the classroom, as teacher Susannah discovers with Kalil:

Susannah, a teacher, waits patiently as Kalil puts on his jacket. It takes three tries to get his left arm in the sleeve. Then the zipper slips out of its notch several times. Thinking he might be frustrated, Susannah asks if Kalil wants help. He keeps working and, on the sixth try, he closes it. "I did it!" he says. "You worked hard to zip it yourself," Susannah acknowledges.

Key Developmental Indicators

HighScope has six **key developmental indicators (KDIs)** in Approaches to Learning: 1. Initiative, 2. Planning, 3. Engagement, 4. Problem solving, 5. Use of resources, and 6. Reflection.

Chapters 3–8 discuss the knowledge and skills young children acquire in each of these KDIs and the specific teaching strategies adults can use to support their development. At the end of each chapter is a scaffolding chart with examples of what children might say and do at early, middle, and later stages of development, and how adults can scaffold their learning through appropriate support and gentle extensions. These charts offer additional ideas on how you might carry out the strategies in the following chapters during play and other interactions with children.

Key Developmental Indicators in Approaches to Learning

A. Approaches to Learning

1. Initiative: Children demonstrate initiative as they explore their world.

Description: Children are eager to learn. They exhibit curiosity, independence, and self-direction as they learn about relationships, materials, actions, and ideas. They take reasonable risks as they investigate the environment.

2. Planning: Children make plans and follow through on their intentions.

Description: Children make plans and decisions, and express choices and intentions based on their interests. Their plans increase in detail and complexity. Children follow through on their plans.

3. Engagement: Children focus on activities that interest them.

Description: Children sustain involvement and concentration in their play. They are persistent, motivated, and able to stay engaged.

4. Problem solving: Children solve problems encountered in play.

Description: Children are inventive and flexible in solving a variety of problems. They progress from using trial and error to more systematic attempts at problem solving.

5. Use of resources: Children gather information and formulate ideas about their world.

Description: Children use all their senses and a variety of tools to explore and gather information about the world around them. They ask questions and try to explain their ideas about the things they encounter.

6. Reflection: Children reflect on their experiences.

Description: Children use their experiences to draw conclusions about people, materials, events, and ideas. They make connections between what they already know and what they are doing and learning.

CHAPTER 3

KDI 1. Initiative

A. Approaches to Learning
1. Initiative: Children demonstrate initiative as they explore their world.

Description: Children are eager to learn. They exhibit curiosity, independence, and self-direction as they learn about relationships, materials, actions, and ideas. They take reasonable risks as they investigate the environment.

At outside time, Marco watches an ant carry a bread crumb twice its size across a patch of dirt. "He's awful little," he comments. "I wonder how he moves something bigger than him." He crouches and continues to study the ant.

❖

Dina helps Kelly open the battery compartment of a camera when he asks her for help. She looks over the camera's back and sides for a switch, finds it, and pops the compartment open.

How Initiative Develops

The landmark publication *Eager to Learn: Educating Our Preschoolers* from the National Research Council (2001) emphasizes that young children are highly motivated to learn. Beginning in infancy, they seek out and master new challenges on their own; no one has to "make" them learn. The initiative to explore the world comes from within and is intrinsically rewarding. As early childhood consultant Marilou Hyson (2008) says in the title of her book on approaches to learning, young learners are "enthusiastic and engaged." They are motivated to learn new things — to explore, exercise mastery and control, and discover the effects of their actions on the environment — even when they are not externally rewarded (Stipek, 2002).

Preschool children show initiative when they choose to participate in a variety of activities that, over time, engage all their senses. They are increasingly comfortable trying new things, taking risks, and generating their own ideas. In a supportive environment, young children approach tasks with growing levels of originality, flexibility, imagination, and confidence. They discuss a broadening range of topics, share observations and ideas, entertain open-ended questions, and solve problems. Preschoolers are more apt to engage fully in activities that support child initiative.

Teaching Strategies That Support Initiative

To promote initiative and build on young children's curiosity and enthusiasm for learning, adults can use the following teaching strategies.

Focus on effort, not outcome

Encourage investigation and celebrate children's attempts, not whether they succeed or fail in their efforts. Emphasize the inherent satisfaction of learning rather than rewarding performance or results. Acknowledge when children try to master a new skill, solve a problem, or explain something they observe. For example, simply state what you see them do or repeat their explanation in an interested voice:

At outside time, Carla's teacher says to her, "You're pumping with all your might to make the swing go up and down."

Use encouragement rather than praise to focus on children's actions (and not on whether they are pleasing adults), and ask open-ended questions so you can listen to children's thinking and help them understand that there is not only one right answer:

At work time, Jack, Sam, and Stacy are in the block area, wondering how to make their cars go faster down the ramp they just built. Jack suggests pushing the cars harder from the top. Sam says, "My uncle has a red car and it goes really fast. Let's use the red one." Stacy thinks the cars will go faster if the ramp is higher. Their teacher says, "How could we find out?" and together they try each child's idea. When the children add blocks at the head of the ramp, Jack exclaims "That did it!" "But only if you use the red car," maintains Sam.

Acknowledge when children try new things

Encourage — but never force — children to explore new materials (scissors, the computer), try out their knowledge and skills (sort beads, ride a trike), or share their idea or opinion (about why ice melts or the feelings an artist is trying to convey). Acknowledge and appreciate the risks children take, whether they are physical or psychological. Taking the initiative requires

"I see that you are now hammering the watch on top," this teacher observes, as she acknowledges the new way the young child is trying to break open the watch.

confidence and trust. Let children know that you see and value their courage as well as their curiosity, as these teachers demonstrate:

At small-group time, the children are using finger paint. Jane is reluctant to touch "icky" things, so the teacher offers her disposable gloves. After a few minutes, Jane removes a glove and dips a forefinger into the paint. She holds it up for the teacher to see. "You put your finger in the paint," the teacher acknowledges. Jane rubs the fingers on that hand together, then wipes them off with a towel. She continues dipping and wiping for the rest of small-group time.

❖

At large-group time, John suggests everyone swing their arms like elephants. He demonstrates and his face lights up when the others imitate this movement. He says to his teacher, "We're all being elephants!" She replies, "Everyone is swinging their arms just like you showed us."

❖

At work time, Sofia and Jacob look at an art book with their teacher Monica. Sofia points to a picture and says, "I like this one because it has lots of red. Red is my most best color." Jacob whispers his favorite color is purple. Monica says, "Let's look for other pictures with red and purple." "Here's a purple one!" Jacob says a little louder when he turns a page and sees one.

Balance freedom and structure in the physical environment

Children take the initiative when the learning environment is designed to provide thoughtful variety in an organized setting. An overly structured classroom can be inhibiting; children may be afraid of "messing up" the order posed by adults. By contrast, a disorganized (chaotic)

setting or an overabundance of materials to choose from can be overwhelming. Likewise, children should feel free to take reasonable risks without hovering adults, but they also need to know that the equipment and materials are safe and will not cause them harm. When all these extremes are balanced, children can exercise their curiosity without feeling anxious.

Initiative is also supported by giving children independent access to materials. This allows them to act with autonomy as they pursue self-directed goals. To balance both freedom and structure, adults can arrange the learning environment to help establish the find-use-return cycle (see the description on the facing page), which gives children greater access to *all* the materials.

Adults should also adapt how the room is arranged as well as the equipment and materials used to stock it to support children with a wide range of abilities (Dowling & Mitchell, 2007). (See "Supporting Initiative in Children With a Wide Range of Abilities" on p. 25).

Encourage children's initiative during adult-initiated parts of the day

Although the daily routine offers both child- and adult-initiated components, children are encouraged to act independently during teacher-guided times of the day. Adults provide materials and/or the originating idea, but then children are free to use materials as they choose and suggest their own ideas. For example, at small-group time, the teacher might introduce materials with a very brief story or demonstration ("Here are the pebbles, leaves, and twigs we collected yesterday on our walk") but then encourages the children to explore and combine them according to their own interests and curiosity ("I wonder what you can make with them").

In the following anecdote, Mariah provides the children with yellow, red, and blue

The Find-Use-Return Cycle

Arranging and labeling the learning environment so that children have easy access to materials helps establish the **find-use-return cycle.**

Find: Similar materials, which are stored together, are kept within easy sight and reach in the room so children can find and get what they want to use.

Use: Children use the materials they have chosen and add more materials as needed to expand on their play ideas.

Return: At cleanup time, children know where to return the materials because they are in clearly labeled containers and similarly labeled shelves.

counting bears during small-group time and then observes how the children explore them in different ways:

At small-group time, Jenny separates the red and yellow bears into two piles. Mark matches one red bear to each blue bear and counts, "One, two, four, four, five." Cory makes a row of alternating yellow and blue bears from one end of the table to the other. Samantha creates a circle using every color and says, "Who wants to ride on my merry-go-round?"

Likewise, at large-group time, adults start a movement, music, or story to act out, and then encourage children to contribute their own ideas on how to move ("Let's all hop up and down"), what to sing ("Do the boat song"), or what situations to add to the story ("We're fish monsters who eat up all the food"):

At large-group time, the teacher plays musical selections that vary in tempo. During the fast song, Craig jumps up and down. "I'm a hopping bug," he says. Gracie slides across the room and says, "This is my speed skating." When the music changes, Craig slows down and comments, "My hopping bug is tired." He pretends to fall asleep. Gracie stops to listen to the change in music, then sways her body while standing in place. "This is my slow dance," she explains.

For examples of how children at different stages of development demonstrate initiative, and how adults can scaffold their learning in this key developmental indicator (KDI), see "Ideas for Scaffolding KDI 1. Initiative" on page 27. The ideas suggested in the chart will help you support and gently extend children's initiative as you play and interact with them in other ways throughout the daily routine.

During this large-group time, the teacher started a movement and then encouraged the children to contribute their own ideas for movement.

Supporting Initiative in Children With a Wide Range of Abilities

- Leave wide aisles for wheelchairs, walkers, and other mobility devices; make sure floors are nonsnag and nonskid (e.g., avoid area rugs and waxed surfaces).

- Provide adaptive equipment and materials for children who need mobility or sensory support.

- Modify materials and activities so children can participate as independently as possible (e.g., use large-type print; easily grasped materials with nonslip handles; enhanced volume; vibrations to accompany or replace sounds; classroom directions for children in more than one modality, such as telling and demonstrating).

- Provide information and experiences in many sensory modalities (e.g., provide visual and auditory cues, use facial expressions and gestures, make daily routine charts tactile by using actual objects and raised shapes and letters, make models with clay and play dough).

- Provide adult assistance as needed when children begin an activity, then reduce support as children show eagerness and ability to act independently.

- Provide opportunities for interaction between peers of differing abilities throughout the program day; treat everyone as equal members of the classroom community.

- Engage children to act as models, helpers, and friends. Acknowledge when children provide assistance and encouragement to one another.

- Encourage children to suggest ideas on how to create or modify activities so they can participate.

Provide opportunities for children of differing abilities to interact with each other.

Encourage all children to participate as independently as possible in daily activities.

During one small-group time, the teacher provided the children with play dough and then supported them in whatever way they used the material.

Ideas for Scaffolding KDI 1. Initiative

Always support children at their current level and occasionally offer a gentle extension.

Earlier	Middle	Later
Children may	*Children may*	*Children may*
• Prefer to use only familiar materials. • Watch others at large-group time. • Use materials the same way they see another child use them at small-group time.	• Explore a new material in one or two ways (e.g., poke their fingers in clay). • Copy another child's action at large-group time. • Add a variation to the way they see another child use materials at small-group time.	• Explore a new material in several ways (e.g., pound, poke, roll, and press a fork into clay). • Lead an action at large-group time. • Try out their own ideas at small-group time.
To support children's current level, adults can	*To support children's current level, adults can*	*To support children's current level, adults can*
• Make materials available but not force children to use them. • Wait for children to enter group activities in their own way and at their own pace. • Acknowledge children's efforts to repeat an action (e.g., "You matched two red bears the same as me").	• Imitate children's actions with materials (e.g., pinch or roll clay). • Acknowledge children's group participation (e.g., "You're touching your toes too"). • Comment on and copy children's variations (e.g., "You did it with three reds. Let me try that").	• Provide additional tools for children to explore materials, such as a garlic press, cookie cutter, or rubber mallet. • Encourage others to follow a child's initiative (e.g., "Ofelia says we should pat our knees"). • Ask children how to do what they did (e.g., "How can I make one that looks like yours?").
To offer a gentle extension, adults can	*To offer a gentle extension, adults can*	*To offer a gentle extension, adults can*
• Use new materials themselves (e.g., poke the clay). • Invite children to join in once the activity is underway by smiling and extending a hand. • Ask children what they think they will do next (e.g., "What are you going to do with the third bear?").	• Draw children's attention to what another child is doing (e.g., "Alicia is using the shell to make prints in her clay"). • Try variations on children's ideas and see how they respond (e.g., "Now I'm wiggling my toes"). • Make a mistake imitating children and see if they correct the error. If not, say "This doesn't look right. Can you help me fix it?"	• Encourage children to use familiar tools in a different way. • Encourage children to verbalize as well as demonstrate ideas to the group. • Pose a new challenge (e.g., "I wonder how else you could do that").

CHAPTER 4

KDI 2. Planning

A. Approaches to Learning
2. Planning: Children make plans and follow through on their intentions.

Description: Children make plans and decisions, and express choices and intentions based on their interests. Their plans increase in detail and complexity. Children follow through on their plans.

Petey plans to work at the computers. When he gets there, he sees that all of the computers are in use, so he goes to the house area. "I'm going to be the pizza delivery guy," he decides.

❖

Simone says she is going to the snow (in the texture table) first and mix it with water, then she is going to make some spaghetti with play dough, and then she will do some painting with orange and green.

To play an active role in their own learning, children must think of themselves as doers — they must have confidence in their ability to make plans and act purposefully to carry them out. At the same time, they need to see adults and other children as respecting their choices and, when necessary, providing assistance to help achieve them. Children's plans reflect what is meaningful and interesting to them, whether it is working with certain materials, practicing a large- or fine-motor skill, reading a book, or pretending with a friend.

The role of planning is gaining increasing attention in the early childhood field. The High-Scope Training for Quality Study (Epstein, 1993) found that "opportunities to plan, carry out, and review activities of their own choosing were positively associated with almost all aspects of children's social, cognitive, and motor development" (p. 152). Many state standards, as well as the Head Start Program Performance Standards (US Department of Health and Human Services, 2002), now include planning in both program and child outcome dimensions.

Too often, however, child planning is seen as being synonymous with children making choices. In her article on planning and reflection in young children, Ann Epstein (2003) emphasizes the distinction: "Planning is more than making choices. Planning is *choice with intention.* That is, the chooser begins with a specific goal or purpose in mind that results in the choice" (p. 29). When children plan, they identify a goal and then consider their options for achieving it, including "what they will do, where they will do it, what materials they will use, who they will do it with, how long it will take, and whether they will need help" (p. 29).

How Planning Develops

As described in chapter 8 of *The HighScope Preschool Curriculum* (Epstein & Hohmann, 2012), planning requires that children be able to hold a mental image of objects and actions in their mind. For younger children who are still tied to the here and now, it helps to see and even hold the options available to them as they take that

To support children's planning, HighScope teachers set up a consistent planning time at a consistent place (e.g., a table for small-group time). Here this child "fishes" for the classroom area she plans to play in at work time.

first step of imagining what they would like to do. Older children can more easily picture the areas, objects, and people in the room; remember what they did the day before; and think about what they want to do next.

Children's plans also become increasingly detailed and complex with development. They may begin with nothing more than a toy they want to use. Over time, they are able to specify a broader range of materials or ideas they intend to work with, the ways in which they

will combine things, the problems they might encounter and the solutions they will try, the sequence of events, or how they can collaborate with others to carry out and elaborate on their initial plans. With experience and development, preschoolers are increasingly able to verbalize, detail, and follow through on their plans. They also grow in their ability not only to plan on their own but also to plan together with a friend. In the later preschool years or early elementary school, they begin to plan with a small group.

Teaching Strategies That Support Planning

The following adult support strategies will help children make plans and act with purpose and intentionality in their play. (For additional strategies to support planning, see chapter 8 in *The HighScope Preschool Curriculum*, Epstein & Hohmann, 2012).

Establish a consistent planning time in the daily routine

HighScope teachers set up a predictable schedule, with a designated planning time, in which children make plans and carry them out every day:

At planning time, Ashlyn points with the magic wand to the areas where she will play. She points to the house area and then to the toy area. "I want to use the Magna-Tiles," she says.

Once they learn this routine, and are secure that they will have the time and materials to act on their intentions, children often make plans before they even get to school:

On the way to school, Lisa tells her mother she is going to play in the house area with Margaret. They will make pizza with cheese and butterscotch chips. She knows exactly what she is going to use to make it. The small brown pebbles the class gathered on their walk yesterday will be the butterscotch pieces. The Styrofoam pellets her mother brought in last week (used to wrap the family's new dishes) will be the cheese. "But not too much cheese," she says to her mother.

Provide opportunities for intentional choices throughout the day

In addition to the scheduled planning time, HighScope programs encourage young children

Adults provide children with the materials for small-group times, but it is up to the children to decide how to use them.

to make intentional choices and decisions throughout the day. For example, while teachers select and give materials to children at small-group time, the children then explore them in their own way. Similarly, children invent variations to move their bodies or make up rhymes and verses at large-group time and transitions. Outside time is another segment of the day when the children decide what equipment to use and with whom they want to play.

Opportunities for Children to Make Choices Throughout the Day

Greeting circle
- Whom to sit with
- What book to look at
- Whom to talk with
- What to talk about

Planning time
- What to do at work time
- What materials to use
- How to use materials
- Where to use materials
- Whom to work with

Work time
- How to begin to carry out their plans
- How to modify plans
- How long to stay with an activity
- What materials to add
- How to solve problems
- What to do next

Recall time
- What to share
- What details to include (who, what, where, how, and so on)
- How to share (gestures, words, drawings, and so on)

Small-group time
- Whom to sit next to
- Which materials to use
- What to do with materials
- What to say
- Whether and how to use backup materials
- Whether and how to interact with others

Large-group time
- What songs to sing
- What verses to add
- What movements to try
- Whether to be a leader
- What to add to a story

Outside time
- What equipment and materials to use
- Whom to play with
- How fast or slow to move
- How loud or quiet to be

During outside time, children have lots of opportunities to make choices. This young child decides to sit on the steps of the climber and drop small bouncing balls to see which one bounces the highest.

Making plans is fundamental to a child's developing sense of competence and equality. When children have opportunities to plan throughout the day and in different contexts, they acquire increased confidence interacting with adults and peers. They see themselves as respected partners in shaping the ongoing events in their world and know their intentions can make a difference:

At work time at the water table, Delaney says, "I'm putting on a smock so my white shirt won't get wet."

❖

Before cleanup time, Talia makes a plan for the following day and writes it on a sticky note. She draws her teacher's letter link symbol and then a doll stick figure. To her this means that she wants to play with Sylvia (a teacher) in the house area. She posts the note on the bulletin board as a reminder.

❖

At small group, Henry says he is going to put glue on his play dough to make it hard. "Then I'm going to make it squishy again," he explains.

Show interest in the choices and decisions children make

Children are not used to being planners, decision makers, and leaders. Simply because they are children, it is natural and often necessary for adults to make decisions for them, particularly with regard to basic matters of health and safety. That is why it is so important for children to set their own agenda at those times when they can appropriately do so. Making choices about playing and learning is an example of such a time. Children can do this at school, and High-Scope teachers also share ideas with parents about how to encourage child choice at home. Because planning is a new experience for young children, it is particularly critical that adults support their endeavors in this process. Adults support children's intentions by commenting on their ideas, repeating and extending their thoughts, imitating their actions, accepting their suggestions, and letting them be the leaders:

At planning time, Allie tells Chris (the teacher) that during work time she wants Chris to call her on the "number phone." She says her number is "2264." Chris pushes those numbers on the phone, but instead of answering, Allie says, "You have the wrong number. Try again." Chris does and Allie picks up the phone.

For examples of how children at different stages of development engage in planning, and how adults can scaffold their learning in this key developmental indicator (KDI), see "Ideas for Scaffolding KDI 2. Planning" on page 35. Use the additional ideas in the chart to help you carry out the strategies described previously to support and gently extend children's planning during play and other daily interactions with them.

Ideas for Scaffolding KDI 2. Planning

Always support children at their current level and occasionally offer a gentle extension.

Earlier	Middle	Later
Children may	*Children may*	*Children may*
• Point to a material they would like to use or play with. • Say the area they want to work in. • Make a plan and then do something else.	• Name the area where they plan to play and name one or two materials. • Plan to work with the same set of materials or repeat the same activities with no variation day after day. • Begin carrying out their plan but then move to other areas or activities.	• Make a detailed plan including the area, materials, actions, and/or other people they will work with. • Plan to continue and expand on their activity the following day. • Stay with their initial plan for a substantial part of work time.
To support children's current level, adults can	*To support children's current level, adults can*	*To support children's current level, adults can*
• Add words to children's gestures (e.g., "You're going to play in the art area"). • Comment on where children play and what they do (e.g., "You're doing the animal puzzle instead of looking at a book"). • Label the new plan and suggest children say the label at planning time (e.g., "You're playing with blocks. Next time, you could say 'blocks' when you make your plan").	• Ask if there are other materials children might need to carry out their plans. • Acknowledge the changed plan and ask children what their new plan is. • Accept children's plans for repeated use of materials and actions. Provide opportunities to combine materials in new ways at small-group time.	• Acknowledge the details in children's plans; encourage them to elaborate the sequence further (e.g., "What will you do first?"). • Connect children's plans to their activities (e.g., "You and Tim built an airport the whole work time, just like you planned to do"). • At cleanup time, ask where children want to store materials they are still working with; provide or help them make work-in-progress signs.
To offer a gentle extension, adults can	*To offer a gentle extension, adults can*	*To offer a gentle extension, adults can*
• Ask or have children show what materials they will use in the area where they are pointing. • Label details of the child's plan (e.g., "You planned to go to the toy area and you did. You're working with the puzzles. At planning time, that's what you told us you wanted to do"). • Comment on the link between children's plans and actions (e.g., "You wanted to play with blocks and now you're building a tower").	• Ask open-ended questions about children's plans (e.g., "What will you use to build that?" "How long do you think it will take?"). • Encourage children to provide details about their new plan (e.g., what they will do and how). • Draw attention to what other children plan to do with the same materials (e.g., "Darin also wants to use the Legos. He's planning to build a barn with them").	• Ask children if they think they will encounter any problems carrying out their plan. • Ask children to describe how they changed their plans to solve any problems that arose during play. • Ask children what the next step(s) will be in continuing to carry out their plans.

CHAPTER 5

KDI 3. Engagement

Approaches to Learning
3. Engagement: Children focus on activities that interest them.

• •

Description: Children sustain involvement and concentration in their play. They are persistent, motivated, and able to stay engaged.

Dwight stands at the easel, applying blue paint with a wide brush. He paints the same corner over and over until he wears a hole in the paper. He pokes his finger in the hole, dips his brush in the cup, and continues to paint over the same spot. He smiles with satisfaction.

❖

At planning time, Felix and Yolanda announce they are going to feed the fish. They bring the box of flakes and a small spoon to the tank, where their teacher helps them measure out the food. For the next 20 minutes, they stare at the fish, commenting excitedly each time one eats and discussing their colors and movements. Other children periodically watch with them before moving on, but Felix and Yolanda keep their eyes glued to what is happening in the fish tank.

How Engagement Develops

Engagement is the "action-oriented dimension of approaches to learning" and includes *attention* and *persistence* (Hyson, 2008, p. 17). *Attention* is focusing one's mental energy on a person, task, or situation, and it is a critical process in *executive function* (Rothbart, Sheese, & Posner, 2007; Zelazo, Muller, Frye, & Marcovitch, 2003; see also "What Is Executive Functioning?" on p. 40). Typically, when adults talk about children and attention, they are often referring to "paying attention" — getting the child to listen to what a grown-up or peer is saying. HighScope prefers the term *engagement* to emphasize that the goal is helping children remain involved with activities and events that interest them. Sustained engagement leads to ongoing discovery, which results in more learning than does merely paying attention to something an adult is saying or doing.

Persistence means staying with an activity in the face of distractions or setbacks. Like problem

solving, it requires an ability to tolerate frustration and to work through challenges to achieve a desired outcome. Attention and persistence are important factors in school readiness (Fantuzzo, Perry, & McDermott, 2004). They require self-regulation, which researchers Elena Bodrova and Deborah Leong (2007) describe as children's "ability to act in a deliberate planned manner in governing much of their own behavior" (p. 127). When they remain engaged, children are satisfying one set of emotions (e.g., the satisfaction of learning or accomplishing a goal) rather than giving into a competing set of needs (such as the impulsive gratification of an immediate reward or the elimination of stress by walking away from a problem).

Differences in engagement are evident from birth and reflect innate temperamental differences. However, there are also clear developmental patterns. Put simply, the older children get, the longer they are able to sustain their attention, working and playing with persistence. They are less susceptible to distractions. The more children engage with the people and tasks before them, the more they learn about their characteristics. The more they learn, in turn, the greater their curiosity to continue learning. Engagement thus becomes self-reinforcing and perpetuating. It cannot be forced, however. Attention and persistence are internally motivated. Children — like adults — seek out and respond to people, materials, and situations that elicit their interest and involvement.

Teaching Strategies That Support Engagement

A primary goal of early education is helping children settle into, focus on, and carry out their intentions in a meaningful and satisfying way. The longer children stay with an activity, the more they learn from the extended time with materials and the enhanced opportunity to reflect on their experience. The following strategies will help young children increase and sustain their level of engagement.

Children become engaged when they are provided materials and experiences that interest them.

What Is Executive Functioning?

The executive functions are a set of processes that all have to do with managing oneself and one's resources in order to achieve a goal. It is an umbrella term for the neurologically based skills involving mental control and self-regulation. The executive functions serve a *command and control* function; they can be viewed as the *conductor* of all cognitive skills. Executive functions help you manage life tasks of all types. For example, executive functions let you organize a trip, a research project, or a paper for school.

Executive functions

1. **Inhibition:** The ability to stop one's own behavior at the appropriate time, including stopping actions and thoughts. The flip side of inhibition is impulsivity; if you have weak ability to stop yourself from acting on your impulses, then you are impulsive.

2. **Shift:** The ability to move freely from one situation to another and to think flexibly in order to respond appropriately to the situation.

3. **Emotional control:** The ability to modulate emotional responses by bringing rational thought to bear on feelings.

4. **Initiation:** The ability to begin a task or activity and to independently generate ideas, responses, or problem-solving strategies.

5. **Working memory:** The capacity to hold information in mind for the purpose of completing a task.

6. **Planning/organization:** The ability to manage current and future-oriented task demands.

7. **Organization of materials:** The ability to impose order on work, play, and storage spaces.

8. **Self-monitoring:** The ability to monitor one's own performance and to measure it against some standard of what is needed or expected.

— Excerpted from Cooper-Kahn & Dietzel (2008, pp. 9–14)

Provide materials and activities that hold children's interest

Attention is not something that can be forced. Children pay attention when they have something worth attending to. For young children, this means materials, interactions, and events that relate to their needs, curiosity, and experiences. By providing an abundance of diverse materials and scheduling a mix of individual and group activities, adults guarantee that each child will find something that engages his or her interest every day. New or reintroduced materials can also attract and sustain attention. They allow children to explore something new in an old way (i.e., see how something learned before applies to an unfamiliar set of materials) and something old in a new way (i.e., apply what they've learned since the last time they used something to explore it in a novel way). A blend of familiarity and novelty allows children to deepen their knowledge and skills.

Finding the right balance of *newness* and *amount* can be tricky, however. Too few materials or repetitive activities can result in boredom. On the other hand, we sometimes overload children with choices to make sure everyone's interest is captured. Observe children to find what works for each individual and for the class as a whole. For example, younger children might intently explore one color of paint — "redness" — at small-group time. Older children may be ready to compare or blend two or more colors. Later still, they may focus on the effects of different painting tools. The following anecdotes illustrate how children respond to the different materials available to them, matching their play to their individual needs for novelty and continuity:

At work time, Vinod goes to the toy area and puts two pieces in a puzzle. He moves to the art area and pokes his fingers in a ball of play dough, then heads to the house area where he watches Jim and Ellie "cook" beads in a plastic bowl. For 10 minutes, Vinod brings them beads, counting bears, and other objects. "Can I stir it?" he asks them when the bowl is full.

❖

At small-group time, Marissa counts the drops of white paint she adds to each cup of red. She puts one drop in the first cup, two drops in the second, and so on, until she has five cups of varying tints. Then she paints a stripe of each color on her paper. "This is the most light and this is the most dark," she tells her teacher, pointing to either end of the row.

❖

Lars and Erin plan to work together in the block area every day for two weeks. Both have recently returned from family vacations. They build an airport with planes, towers, "takeoff ramps," a food court, and a "suitcase merry-go-round." Every day they add more structures and use materials from other areas of the room, such as long paper strips for runways.

Give children ample time to carry out their intentions

Schedule a daily work time of at least 45 minutes so children have enough time to implement their plans. Even if they do not initially stay with one thing, a long work period sends them the message that their ideas merit sustained activity and that such extended focus has value. Also allow ample time for children to reach a comfortable stopping point at small-group time. Don't push them to finish or move on to the next activity

During work time, this child (and her friends) had ample time to build an elaborate restaurant.

in the day's routine as a whole group. Make the next activity one that children can transition to gradually (such as washing up for snacktime) so children can proceed at their own pace when they are ready. Give them notice when an activity is coming to an end, and provide work-in-progress signs so children can make a plan to continue a work-time or group-time project the next day, as this teacher does with Nia:

At small-group time, Nia makes a pattern of alternating blue and yellow stickers around the border of her paper. When the activity ends, she still has several stickers left and one edge of the paper is blank. She looks upset as one by one the other children head to the rug for large-group time. "Would you like to continue making your pattern tomorrow?" her teacher asks. "Yes," says Nia, looking relieved. She puts her materials on the top of a shelf with a work-in-progress sign and skips to the rug to join her classmates.

By the same token, be sensitive to when children lose interest in a small- or large-group activity. Either modify the activity (e.g., introduce backup materials or have restless children move instead of sing) or bring the activity to an end. If children feel forced to continue, that time period may take on unpleasant associations. They may come to dislike group time in general and refuse to participate, even on those days when the materials and actions would otherwise interest them.

Minimize interruptions and transitions

While it is true that levels of engagement increase with development, it is wrong to assume that young children have short attention spans. In fact, adults may inadvertently hamper children's concentration by assuming they need a constant change of pace or novel stimulation.

To encourage children to maintain their involvement in whatever interests them, it is important to minimize interruptions and transitions throughout the day. For example, during work time, HighScope teachers do not set up a "special project" and pull small groups of children away from their chosen activities to engage in this special one. Instead, children choose whether and when to move on to a different set of activities or actions during work time. Likewise, adults schedule as few transitions as possible between parts of the day. This allows children to settle down and settle into every part of the daily routine, giving each component its due as a worthwhile and engaging activity.

For developmental illustrations of young children's levels of engagement, and how adults can support and gently extend early learning in this key developmental indicator (KDI), see "Ideas for Scaffolding KDI 3. Engagement" on page 43. The ideas suggested in the chart, as well as those detailed previously, will help you scaffold children's engagement as you play and interact with them during the program day.

Ideas for Scaffolding KDI 3. Engagement

Always support children at their current level and occasionally offer a gentle extension.

Earlier	Middle	Later
Children may	*Children may*	*Children may*
• Flit between areas and/or materials. • Stay with an activity that interests them for a short time. • Observe others engaged in a task or activity.	• Explore one or two materials before moving on. • Stay with an activity that interests them for a moderate amount of time. • Enter into an activity that appears engaging to others.	• Become involved with materials. • Stay with an activity that interests them for a long time. • Invite others to sustain or extend an engaging activity (e.g., "Joey, wanna help us build this bridge?").
To support children's current level, adults can	*To support children's current level, adults can*	*To support children's current level, adults can*
• Invite children to join you in an activity related to their interests (e.g., "Jared and Kylie asked me to read them the train book. Would you like to listen too?") • Play alongside children; repeat their words and imitate their actions. • Comment on the materials and activities children are observing; ask if they would like to join in.	• Comment on and describe what children are doing. • Comment on children's sustained attention (e.g., "You worked on your boat painting for quite a while"). • Suggest ways children can become engaged in ongoing play (e.g., "Maybe they need another firefighter to help them carry the heavy hose").	• Use materials in the same variety of ways as the children. • Describe and encourage children to describe what they did in detail. • Ask for children's ideas on how you and others can fit into their play themes (e.g., "I wonder how Joey will help you build the bridge. Oh, I see. He'll hold up the end while you put more blocks underneath").
To offer a gentle extension, adults can	*To offer a gentle extension, adults can*	*To offer a gentle extension, adults can*
• Ask children to suggest the next activity (e.g., the next book to read). • Ask children to describe what they are doing so you can copy them and check to see if you understand them (e.g., "Is this the way to do it?"). • Encourage children to turn to one another for ideas and assistance (e.g., "Maybe Donovan can show you how he does it").	• Encourage children to describe and demonstrate their actions for you. • Add related materials to extend children's play. • Encourage children to think of how they can join and build on the play of others (e.g., "I wonder if there's a way that you can help them").	• Ask open-ended questions and pose challenges to help children extend their involvement with materials. • Encourage children to seek out related materials in other areas of the room. • Encourage children to describe how they each contributed to carrying out their collaborative play idea (e.g., "So Joey brought extra blocks. Then what did you and Sammy do?").

KDI 4. Problem Solving

A. Approaches to Learning
4. Problem solving: Children solve problems encountered in play.

• •

Description: Children are inventive and flexible in solving a variety of problems. They progress from using trial and error to more systematic attempts at problem solving.

When Isaac accidentally tears his painting while removing it from the easel, he lays it on the floor, tapes the torn parts back together, and hangs the painting up to dry.

❖

At outside time, Alana puts her hand on the first rung of the climber and draws back in surprise. "It's wet!" she tells her teacher Becki. "It certainly is wet," Becki agrees. After discovering other parts of the climber are wet too, Alana says, "I'm going to get a towel to wipe off the water." She gets a towel and dries off each rung. "Now I can climb!" she says.

Children who pursue their own initiatives inevitably encounter obstacles in their play. When children are encouraged to solve these problems on their own, they gain valuable opportunities to deal thoughtfully and creatively with unanticipated situations. Allowing children to work through problems rather than jumping in to help them serves two purposes. First, they come to see themselves as competent individuals who can handle situations independently. Second, they form the *problem-solving habit,* a trait that will benefit them throughout their school years and into adulthood.

How Problem Solving Develops

Significant differences in how children approach problem solving emerge early in development. Psychologist Carol Dweck (2002) found that young children fall into two categories: They are either *performance oriented* or *learning (or mastery) oriented.* Children with a performance orientation focus on getting a positive evaluation from others and tend to avoid situations that may result in failure or criticism. They do not persist in solving problems where they are unlikely to succeed. In contrast, children with a learning orientation focus on increasing their abilities, regardless of the feedback from others. They tackle new challenges if they anticipate learning something, even if their initial efforts are not successful. This latter orientation is a better predictor of achievement. Although approaches to problem solving are affected by such temperamental differences, children's behavior is also influenced by whether adults emphasize outcomes (performance) or efforts (learning).

In addition to individual differences, there are also developmental changes. Younger children approach problems with more enthusiasm

Younger children are enthusiastic problem solvers, like these two children, who are building a tower with nesting blocks.

and self-confidence but less persistence. Older children are more persistent and flexible, and are likely to propose their own ideas and solutions (Flavell, Miller, & Miller, 2001). Self-regulation also plays a role. Studies of *executive function* (also called *effortful control*) show that older children are better able to regulate their attention and apply their cognitive skills in problem-solving situations (Zelazo, Muller, Frye, & Marcovitch, 2003). The years between three and five are especially important in the development of these executive functions because of concurrent changes in brain development, particularly in the frontal cortex, which is responsible for regulating and expressing emotion (Shore, 2003).

Teaching Strategies That Support Problem Solving

Adults can encourage children to solve problems on their own in the following ways.

Encourage children to describe the problems they encounter

When you see a child having a problem, hold back to let the child recognize and describe the situation. This first step helps children develop the ability to arrive at a solution. Children may not see problems in the same way as an adult, but it is more important for them to have the opportunity to view and describe it in their own words. In doing so, they begin to trust their skills as observers and analyzers. Not only is this process central to positive emotional development, it also lies at the heart of scientific thinking and reasoning, as demonstrated by Cole's description of his problem with the computer:

Cole comes to his teacher Jackie and says, "The computer's not working." She asks him to tell her how it isn't working and follows him back to the computer. "See, it keeps going back to where I started," he explains. When Jackie asks Cole what he wants the computer to do, he says, "Go to the next part of the game." She looks at the screen, points to the arrow icons, and says, "I wonder what these do?" Coles tries clicking on the icons. When he clicks on the → icon, the game advances. Cole says, "Now I got it working!"

Early in their development, children may not be able to identify or verbalize problems. They may only have a vague sense that something is preventing them from carrying out their intentions. In such cases, simply state the problem for the child. If you use phrases such as "So the problem is…," children will eventually get the idea of identifying a problem in order to figure out a solution:

At work time in the house area, Ariel's teacher says, "It looks like you want to wear your necklace. So the problem is that it's too short to fit over your head." Ariel's eyes light up and she says, "Yeah. Maybe I can add some more yarn to make it bigger — bigger like my head."

Give children time to come up with their own solutions

Just as HighScope adults wait patiently for children to identify problems, they also hold back so children can figure out how to solve them:

At work time in the art area, when Hank's glue bottle is clogged, Alison (another child) tries squeezing it very hard. She tries unclogging the bottle with a nail, then finally gets a new glue bottle for Hank.

❖

At work time in the block area, when Matthew wants the big two-sided ramp that someone else is using, he makes his own ramp by taping two single ramps together.

While the adult's solution may be more efficient or effective, simply giving it to the child would deprive the child of an opportunity to learn and develop confidence in his or her problem-solving abilities.

Talk with children about what is and is not working

To help children move from trial and error to more systematic attempts at problem solving, adults can encourage them to describe and think about the results of their actions. They can make comments and ask open-ended questions to help children consider other alternatives. It is just as important for children to be aware of when a solution works as it is for them to

recognize when a different approach is needed, as shown in this conversation between Peter and his caregiver Neenah:

Peter is doing a puzzle. He has most of the pieces in place, but no matter how he turns the remaining ones, he cannot make them fit the spot for the elephant's ear. "You tried all the pieces and none of them fit," says his caregiver Neenah. "I turned and turned them," says Peter with a sigh. "I wonder if you have all the pieces," says Neenah, spotting one on the floor behind him. They search together. "Look what I found," says Peter. He slides it into the empty spot. "I did it!" he proudly tells Neenah. "Yes, you found the missing piece," she says.

Conversing with children about what they did and why it did (or did not) solve the problem helps to establish a cause-and-effect connection in their mind. Once they have this mental association, they are more likely to apply a solution to similar problems in the future.

Assist children who are frustrated

Sometimes children do need adult help, especially when their inability to solve a problem keeps them from moving forward with their plans. HighScope teachers are alert to when children have tried to solve a problem and run into roadblocks they cannot get past on their own. At this point, adults step in to provide just enough assistance for children to either continue with a solution on their own or proceed to carry out their intentions. Teachers provide a brief explanation in such cases so children can learn from the experience and perhaps use the information on their own later:

While Ashlyn is in the woodworking area, the drill bit comes off the drill she is using. She pushes it back in place, but it keeps falling out.

These two children are trying to make a bucket pulley.

Their teacher talks with them about what is and is not working with the pulley.

The children problem-solved together to make a real working bucket pulley!

Ashlyn brings it to her teacher, Chris, and asks her to "fix it." Chris tightens the bit in the drill and says, "Sometimes I have to tighten it like this for it to stay." Ashlyn proceeds with her plan to make a dinosaur bed.

For developmental examples of problem solving, and how adults can scaffold young children's learning in this key developmental indicator (KDI), see "Ideas for Scaffolding KDI 4. Problem Solving" on page 51. Use the additional ideas in the chart to support and gently extend children's problem-solving skills as you play and interact with them throughout the daily routine.

Once children have experience problem-solving with adult support, they often will use the same problem-solving strategies with their peers, such as working together to build a tall tower of Legos that won't fall down.

Ideas for Scaffolding KDI 4. Problem Solving

Always support children at their current level and occasionally offer a gentle extension.

Earlier	Middle	Later
Children may	*Children may*	*Children may*

Earlier	Middle	Later
• Ignore (not recognize or not acknowledge) a problem with materials. • Play with materials until a problem arises (i.e., not anticipate potential problems). • Express frustration in words or gestures when encountering a problem with materials (e.g., throw materials on the floor, cry, walk away).	• Recognize a problem with materials and ask for help solving it. • Anticipate potential problems in play (e.g., there may not be enough big blocks to build the skyscraper). • Try one or two ways to solve a problem with materials.	• Describe a problem with materials either spontaneously or when asked. • Anticipate solutions to potential problems (e.g., "If there's no room at the computers, I'll do a puzzle until it's my turn"). • Solve or try three or more ways to solve a problem with materials.
To support children's current level, adults can	*To support children's current level, adults can*	*To support children's current level, adults can*
• Help children identify problems (e.g., "It looks like the string is too short to reach to the other side"). • Label problems for children when they arise in play. • Acknowledge children's feelings; be alert to signs of frustration, and offer help before they become upset.	• Encourage children to describe the problem (e.g., "Show/tell me what isn't working"). • Acknowledge when children anticipate problems (e.g., "You think there may not be enough"). • Offer suggestions (e.g., "Sometimes when I have the same problem, I turn it like this").	• Encourage children to elaborate (e.g., "Show/tell me which buttons you pushed and what happened"). • Encourage children to think of challenges they might face in carrying out their plans and how they could prevent or solve them. • Acknowledge children's problem-solving attempts, whether or not they succeed (e.g., "You tried three kinds of tape before you found one strong enough to hold it in place").
To offer a gentle extension, adults can	*To offer a gentle extension, adults can*	*To offer a gentle extension, adults can*
• Encourage children to provide more information about the problem (e.g., "Which part isn't working?"). • Encourage children to identify potential problems when they plan (e.g., "Do you think you'll have enough red stickers to go all the way around?"). • Add vocabulary words (e.g., frustrated, out of patience, annoyed it's not working) to help children describe and express their frustration.	• Encourage children to turn to one another for assistance (e.g., "Maybe Jada can show you how she got the computer to play the song"). • Ask for children's ideas to solve potential problems (e.g., "What could you do if that happens?"). • Ask what else children might try (e.g., "What else could you use?" "Could you do something else with it that might work?").	• Encourage children to explain what they think is causing the problem. • Ask children why they think their proposed solution will work. • Ask children to explain why what they tried did or did not work.

KDI 5. Use of Resources

A. Approaches to Learning

5. Use of resources: Children gather information and formulate ideas about their world.

Description: Children use all their senses and a variety of tools to explore and gather information about the world around them. They ask questions and try to explain their ideas about the things they encounter.

Two children are playing under a shade tree. They run to the flower bed, where their teacher and several classmates are digging for worms. "Look at our toes!" they say as they point to the dark tips of their shoes. With the children's permission, the teacher and their classmates touch their feet. "They're wet!" declares one child. They all run over to feel the wet grass under the tree.

❖

At greeting time, one child announces, "I got new shoes with laces." The other children comment that their shoes have straps, buckles, Velcro strips, and so on. They get interested in what makes shoes stay on their feet and talk about how fasteners work in general.

Young children become increasingly adept at using resources in their environment — manipulable objects, observable processes, and human expertise — to add to their growing body of knowledge. According to early childhood educator Lilian Katz (1993), the dispositions or "habits of mind" they bring to this endeavor include a desire to find things out, make sense of their experiences, strive for accuracy, and be empirical (i.e., guided by practical experience). Preschoolers are the original "show me" population. They look for objects, actions, and events that confirm their own and others' ideas.

How Use of Resources Develops

Although there are temperamental differences in children's willingness to try new experiences (Kagan, 2005), there is also a developmental trend toward greater openness. That is, older children are generally more willing than younger children to try something new and different. Preschoolers explore an expanding array of equipment, tools, and materials, using all their senses not only to observe but also to make connections between emerging areas of knowledge. Research on the neural networks formed in the brain during these years finds that "by the time the child is three or four years of age, there has already developed an enormously complex and interlinked knowledge base about the world" (Catherwood, 1999, p. 33). Moreover, the more they know, the more adept young children become at extracting knowledge from the resources around them. They bring greater depth and flexibility to their explorations, alert to the multiple possibilities for learning.

There is also a difference in the kinds of questions three- and four-year-olds ask. Unlike the reflexive "*what* is that?" inquiry of a toddler, a preschooler's "*why* is that?" is more reflective. Because their language skills are increasing, especially the ability to participate in conversational exchanges, preschoolers ask questions that are more appropriate to the circumstances. They think about what they have heard (or seen or felt), attempt to fit this observation into the mental constructs they have formed about similar objects or situations, and then strive to reconcile any discrepancies. Preschoolers may ask questions aloud ("Why does it get cold when it snows?") or hold an internal conversation with themselves ("I wonder if tape will work better than glue; let me try it"). They use the people and materials available to them to help answer their inquiries.

The importance of providing young children with age-appropriate and hands-on resources to draw on during these investigations cannot be overstated. The HighScope Training for Quality Study (Epstein, 1993) found that in addition to opportunities for planning and reflection, access to diverse materials was the most significant predictor of early development. The more programs provided a variety of resources (print, art supplies, puzzles, music, movement and dramatic play props, blocks and other construction toys, sand and water) and ample time to explore them, the higher children's scores on measures of development, particularly language skills. According to Ann S. Epstein (1993), "language was positively affected by the accessibility of materials and by teacher-child interaction styles. Verbal skills develop when children talk about what and how they are using materials during activities" (p. 152).

Research in non-HighScope as well as HighScope settings supports this finding. For example, an international study of diverse programs in 10 countries, coordinated by HighScope, found that the availability of open-ended materials in the preprimary years was a significant predictor of children's cognitive and language performance at age seven (Montie,

Xiang, & Schweinhart, 2006). These studies are consistent with brain research, which indicates that "the tasks for early years educators [is] facilitating the further articulation and application of that web of knowledge and verbal expression" (Catherwood, 1999, p. 33).

Teaching Strategies That Support Use of Resources

To help children use a variety of materials and tools as they explore and draw conclusions about their world, teachers can use the following strategies.

Provide open-ended materials and experiences that appeal to all the senses

Children are more likely to explore and learn meaningful lessons when classroom materials can be manipulated and experienced in many ways (seen, heard, smelled, touched, and tasted). Closed-ended materials — those with one "correct" use — offer limited possibilities for exploration and discovery. Children quickly lose interest in them. By contrast, open-ended materials — which can be put to multiple uses — sustain children's attention and capture their imagination. (For examples of open-ended materials in use, see pp. 56–57). These types of materials offer many opportunities for manipulation and discovery, often yielding unexpected results. For example, children working with real clay were surprised to see it lighten in color as it dried, unlike play dough. This led them to feel other art materials and compare their moisture content.

Diverse materials and experiences also respect children's individual preferences for learning through one or more particular senses. Just as temperamental differences may be manifested in different emotional styles, so too can children be drawn to the different sensory or

Play dough can be used to form letters or to make a "worm."

Blocks can be used to create a pattern or to build a platform for dancing or modeling dress-up clothes.

Large cardboard tubes can be used as a tunnel for cars or as a "telephone" to speak through.

functional characteristics of objects. Some children gravitate toward visual learning, while others absorb information through auditory or tactile experiences. Most children employ a range of senses in different combinations and degrees. An active learning setting lets them choose the resources that work best for them at any given time. For more on using open-ended materials that appeal to all the senses, see chapter 6 in *The HighScope Preschool Curriculum* (Epstein & Hohmann, 2012).

Talk with children about how they use materials

Brain research indicates that conversing with children as they use materials lets them process their experiences and reflect on what they are learning (for more information on recall time, see chapter 8 of *The HighScope Preschool Curriculum*, Epstein & Hohmann, 2012). Verbalizing their actions and observations helps children make neural connections that appear to have more staying power. It is therefore important for adults to converse with children about the objects and people they choose to help carry out their ideas, the ways in which they problem-solve with these resources, the observations they make (again, using all the senses), and the conclusions they draw, as illustrated in the following dialogue:

Child: *(Constructing a series of towers with square Duplo blocks)* I'm making a lot of trees.

Teacher: You're making trees with the blocks.

Child: I have to make a lot of them.

Teacher: I wonder how many you have to make.

Child: I need seven. *(Points to each stack of blocks and counts them)* One, two, three, four. I have four.

Teacher: You made four trees. Do you think you'll make more?

Child: *(Looking at the remaining blocks in the pile)* I have to make more until I get to seven.

While conversation helps children be more purposeful in their actions and intentional in drawing conclusions, adults should be careful not to talk too much or intrude upon their play. Sometimes children just need uninterrupted time to explore and observe on their own. Adults therefore need to be sensitive to when their comments and questions are unwelcome. At such times, it is best to back off. Simply sit quietly alongside children and observe what they are doing to convey your interest and support their exploration of the resources at hand. Children may choose to initiate conversation at a later point, when they are ready to share what they did and what they observed.

Encourage children to use a variety of resources to answer their own questions

Early childhood educators tend to think about whether and what kind of questions they can ask children, rather than pondering the kinds of questions children ask adults or wondering about the questions that children ask themselves. Yet these questions, because they originate in the children's own interests and observations, lead to the most meaningful and lasting insights. Adults can therefore actively support early learning by encouraging children to ask questions and helping them locate the resources that allow them to find answers. The adult might comment, "I wonder how that would work" as an invitation for the child to experiment with materials and observe the results. Even earlier in the discovery process, a teacher can simply say, "I wonder what you could use to find out" and encourage the child to look around the classroom for (or the teacher might suggest) resources that would be appropriate:

At outside time, Jonathan, Sarah, and Garth dispute whose bucket has the most water. They each look down into their buckets but the amounts are similar, and it is difficult to tell from that

Conversing with children as they use materials enables them to process and reflect on what they are doing.

perspective. "I wonder if there's another way we can find out," says their teacher. "We can measure," says Sarah. "How could we do that?" the teacher asks. After some discussion, the children ask their teacher to help them mark the water level on the outside of their buckets with chalk. The teacher puts her finger on the level, and each child makes a dot or line next to it. Sarah's bucket has the most, followed by Garth's, and then Jonathan's. Garth and Jonathan each add water to their buckets and mark them with chalk until "they are all the same."

For examples of how children at different stages of development make use of resources, and how adults can support and gently extend early learning in this key developmental indicator (KDI), see "Ideas for Scaffolding KDI 5. Use of Resources" on page 61. The chart offers ideas you can use to carry out the strategies described previously in your daily play and other interactions with the children in your program.

Children at a later developmental stage may use multiple materials in elaborate ways. These young children are using play dough, a play stove, and real cooking pots to make a meal that they will invite their friends to eat.

Ideas for Scaffolding KDI 5. Use of Resources

Always support children at their current level and occasionally offer a gentle extension.

Earlier	Middle	Later

Children may

- Explore the properties of a few materials.
- Use one or two materials with a purpose in mind (e.g., tape two paper towel tubes together).
- Ask simple "what" questions (e.g., "What do you call this?").

Children may

- Explore the properties and functions of several materials.
- Combine several materials with a purpose in mind (e.g., make a magic cape by attaching strings to a large piece of fabric).
- Ask "why" and "how" questions (e.g., "Why does it need water to grow?" "How does it light up?").

Children may

- Explore, combine, and compare many materials.
- Combine multiple materials and use them in elaborated ways (e.g., make a bus with chairs and a steering wheel and invite others to ride it).
- Attempt to answer their own questions (e.g., which kinds of tape can lift objects of different weights).

To support children's current level, adults can

- Provide related materials and tools that may be of interest to children.
- Describe, and encourage children to describe, what they are doing with materials.
- Name materials for children.

To support children's current level, adults can

- Label and describe children's actions with materials.
- Ask children how they plan to use various materials in their play.
- Encourage children to describe what they observe.

To support children's current level, adults can

- Add materials to the classroom to extend children's explorations (e.g., factual books about artists or animals).
- Comment on the variety of materials and tools children use in their play.
- Encourage children to answer their own questions.

To offer a gentle extension, adults can

- Provide opportunities to combine or use familiar materials in new ways.
- Ask children if there are other materials that could help them with their plans.
- Encourage children to connect the new things they discover to what they already know.

To offer a gentle extension, adults can

- Encourage children to explore materials in more ways (e.g., "I wonder what it smells like").
- Encourage children to explain how the materials will help them carry out their play ideas.
- Ask children how they could find out the answers to their questions.

To offer a gentle extension, adults can

- Ask children to describe what is the same or different about materials, including appearance, sound, smell, texture, and, if appropriate, taste.
- Encourage children to describe how the properties of materials helped them carry out their intentions (e.g., "How did you know it would stick?").
- Suggest resources children can use to answer their own questions.

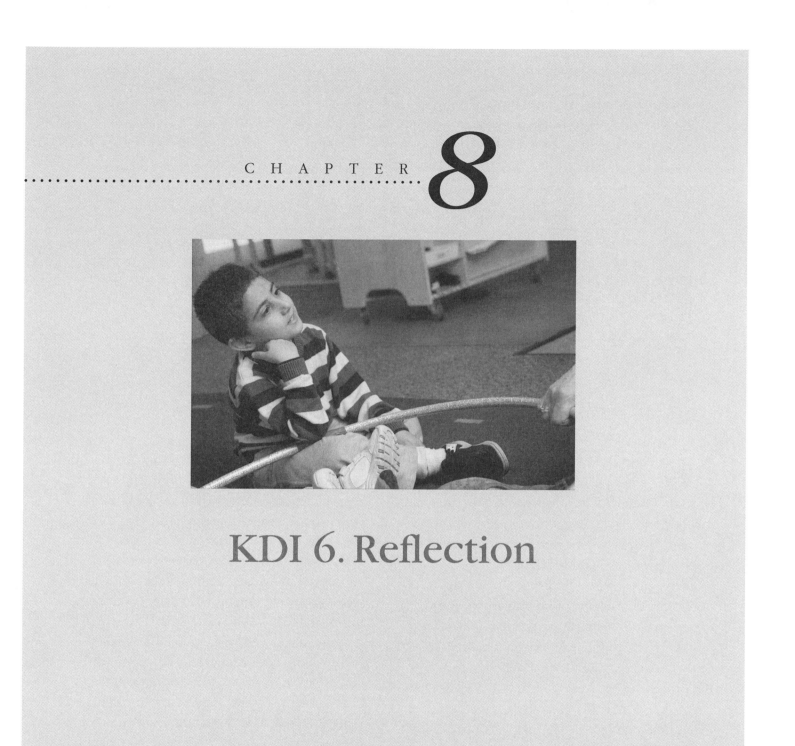

CHAPTER 8

KDI 6. Reflection

A. Approaches to Learning
6. Reflection: Children reflect on their experiences.

Description: Children use their experiences to draw conclusions about people, materials, events, and ideas. They make connections between what they already know and what they are doing and learning.

Sheila asks her teacher Jerome, "Why is David not here today?" Jerome replies that he does not know, and Sheila says, "Maybe he is sick. When I was sick, I didn't come to school."

❖

The children put on their jackets, mittens, hats, and boots to play in the snow. "When I got cold," says Fallon, "Grandma Dee gave me hot chocolate to make me warm again."

Most early childhood practitioners recognize the importance of developing memory skills in young children. However, reflection involves more than "memory or a rote recitation of completed activities. Reflection is *remembering with analysis*" (Epstein, 2003, p. 29). Being reflective goes beyond reporting what one has done. It means actively thinking about one's experiences to better understand how the world works. When children reflect on their actions, they "become aware of what they learned in the process, what was interesting, how they feel about it, and what they can do to build on or extend the experience" (p. 29).

How Reflection Develops

Cognitive and language developments in the preschool years make children increasingly able to engage in reflection. Because three- and four-year olds are beginning to construct mental images (representations) of objects, events, and interactions, they can draw on this information to both review and anticipate. They are becoming less tied to the here and now. These representations allow them to make if-then connections and to contemplate "what if" for situations that haven't actually occurred. Words also help them "encode" past experience in memory so they can use this verbal knowledge base to imagine and articulate a broader range of possibilities and explanations.

Just as children's emerging abilities aid in reflection, opportunities to reflect in turn contribute significantly to other domains of development (Epstein, 1993). The capacity for reflection is also an important foundation for later academic success. Reflection, like planning, is decontextualized language (focused on non-immediate events), which in turn is related to later reading success (Dickinson & Smith, 1994). Early childhood specialist Sue Bredekamp (2010, p. 51) says, "reflecting on and analyzing experiences…are metacognitive processes that build self-regulation and executive functioning," which promote literacy and mathematics (Bodrova &

Leong, 2007). Unlike rote memorization, reflection lets children discover and apply underlying principles. For example, grasping the alphabetic principle that each letter has a unique written representation and sound allows children to apply this knowledge whenever they encounter a new letter. Being able to generalize instead of memorizing a situation-specific piece of information each time (i.e., not having to rediscover that "m" has its own sound just like "k") is a more efficient way to learn.

Sometimes our emphasis on making sure children have diverse materials to work with overlooks the child's equally important need to engage with ideas. Reflection is a higher level process that children "superimpose" upon objects, actions, and interactions. Science educators Karen Worth and Sharon Grollman (2003) note that "direct experience with materials is critical but is not enough. Children also need to reflect on their work. They need to analyze their experiences, think about ideas such as patterns and relationships, try out new theories, and communicate with others. These processes allow children to think in new ways about what they did, how they did it, and what is significant to them" (p. 5).

Teaching Strategies That Support Reflection

In addition to a daily recall time, reflection can and should take place throughout the program day. The following teaching strategies will encourage children to think about their experiences and learn meaningful lessons about the objects, people, and events in their lives. For additional ideas on how to support reflection, see the discussion of recall time in chapter 8 in *The HighScope Preschool Curriculum* (Epstein & Hohmann, 2012).

Establish a consistent recall time in the daily routine

When recall time is a predictable part of the daily routine, immediately following cleanup time, children develop the "habit" of reviewing and thinking about their work-time activities. They adopt it as a way of processing their experiences. Knowing recall time is on the schedule, children might consciously remember something because it will be interesting to share.

Adults can also encourage children to be reflective by using recall-type questions and comments at other times of the day. For example, at small-group time, a teacher might encourage a child to describe how she made a block construction ("Show me how you got this part to balance"), which helps the child imagine and re-create her actions. During work time, the teacher can ask children to recap a pretend-play scenario so she can take on the role they assign her to play ("So I'll be the big sister and the baby brother won't stop crying. What have you already tried doing for him?"). Through these interactions, children will think about their behavior during every part of the daily routine and will, in turn, be able to describe and reflect on their activities in greater detail at recall time itself.

Make comments and ask questions that encourage reflection

Building on the previous strategy, adults can ask open-ended questions and share observations that specifically promote reflection. These include the following:

- "How else could the story end?"
- "What if…?"
- "How else could you have…?"

Questions like these encourage children to reflect on what has already happened in order to

To build connections between previous and current experiences, this teacher comments, "I saw you did the corners first in your last puzzle. In this puzzle, you did the corners and also the sides first, before you did the middle."

consider alternative possibilities, as this anecdote illustrates:

Carlos makes a dinosaur leash by gluing an upright stick to a flat block of wood. When he lifts the stick, the block of wood falls off. Carlos adds more glue, but the block of wood still falls off. He holds the block of wood in his hand. "It's too heavy," he tells his teacher. "Do you see anything else you could use?" she asks. Carlos looks around the room and gets tape from the art area. He wraps it around the leash several times. "There," he says. "That's super tape! It's strong enough to stick it."

Another way adults can help children generalize from their experiences is to make

comments such as "I wonder where else this would work." To build connections between previous and current experiences, adults can ask, "What does this remind you of?" or comment, "I heard you make that 'vroom' sound when you rode the trike outside. Now you are making the same sound while you move your car down the ramp."

Young children solve problems using trial and error and gradually progress to more systematic attempts to find solutions (see chapter 6). Whichever level children are at, adults can encourage them to observe and describe the effects of their actions before they try the next thing. Speculate with them about why a solution did or did not work, and wonder what else they could try based on the outcome ("It's still too short. What will you try next?"). Referring children to their peers for help and asking them to explain their solutions to one another also promotes reflection ("Jonetta got hers to stick. Maybe she can tell you how she did it"). When children are called on to demonstrate or describe their actions, they have to think about what they did in order to communicate it to someone else.

Playing alongside children as partners creates openings for these types of conversations to occur. For example, if a teacher imitates a child, the adult can say, "Show (or tell) me how to build one like yours." Especially for younger children who are just learning to recall, helping them reflect while they are doing something sets the stage for their being able to recall something after a period of time has elapsed. With practice and the development of cognitive capacity, children are progressively able to recall things that happened farther in the past.

Use photographs and mementos to help children remember and reflect on experiences

One meaning of the phrase "a picture is worth a thousand words" is that a single image can evoke the entire story behind it. A sequence of photographs not only helps children recall the order in which things happened but also highlights if-then connections. For example, pictures of children building a block construction not only helps them recall the series of steps but also lets them see how deciding to make a wide base at the beginning meant they needed more blocks for each wall.

Likewise, an object representing an event, such as something brought back from a field trip, can elicit memories of the things, people, and actions surrounding the occasion. In this anecdote, the children use the images on postcards to reflect on the meaning of the artwork they saw at a museum:

The day after the class field trip to the art museum, the children look at the reproduction postcards they bought in the gift shop. One child studies a painting in somber tones and says, "It's gray because he was sad when he made it." Another child examines a metal sculpture of a large figure and comments, "It's so tall, you can't see its eyes. It's scary, like a monster." A third child, rather than reflecting on the art or the time in the museum, remembers the trip to the museum cafeteria. "Tommy spilled his juice on my shoe," the child recalls.

For examples of how children at different stages of development engage in reflection, and how adults can scaffold their learning in this key developmental indicator (KDI), see "Ideas for Scaffolding KDI 6. Reflection" on page 68. Use the ideas in the chart, in addition to those detailed previously, to support and gently extend children's reflection during your play and other interactions with them.

Ideas for Scaffolding KDI 6. Reflection

Always support children at their current level and occasionally offer a gentle extension.

Earlier	Middle	Later
Children may	*Children may*	*Children may*
• Point to or show you something they played with.	• Recall one thing they did with some detail (e.g., "I made a clay dog with eyes").	• Recall and describe one or more things they did in detail (e.g., "The white tape came off, so we used the black tape and stuck the blanket to the table to make our cave").
• Recall a material they used or one thing they did (e.g., "Computer" or "Played boat").	• Connect related experiences (e.g., when one child describes a family camping trip, say "We went camping on our vacation too").	
• Tell something they did closely connected to the event (e.g., say the last thing they did at work time).	• Connect what the children did at work time to their initial plan.	• Say what was the same and/or different about an experience (e.g., "When we went camping, we slept in a tent, not a trailer").
		• Act based on a previous experience (e.g., put on a smock because last time their clothes got wet).
To support children's current level, adults can	*To support children's current level, adults can*	*To support children's current level, adults can*
• Ask what else children played with.	• Add details about what they observed children doing at work time.	• Ask children to show what they did and explain how they did it.
• Restate and add to what the children said in a sentence (e.g., "You made a boat with the blocks").	• Acknowledge children's awareness of similarities in their experiences.	• Ask what else was the same or different about two experiences.
• Add a time frame to what the children said (e.g., "The last thing you played with before cleanup time was the Legos").	• Remind children of their initial plan as they recall their work-time activities (e.g., show them what they drew, replay what they said).	• Describe the connections between children's past experiences and their current actions.
To offer a gentle extension, adults can	*To offer a gentle extension, adults can*	*To offer a gentle extension, adults can*
• Ask children to describe what they did with the materials they point to.	• Encourage children to add details to their descriptions of what they did (e.g., "How did you make the dog's eyes?").	• Add vocabulary words to elaborate on children's descriptions (e.g., "So the electrician's tape was stronger").
• Ask what else children remember about an experience (e.g., "Did you do anything else with the blocks?").	• Encourage children to describe additional similarities in their experiences (e.g., "Tell me about your sleeping bags").	• Wonder what might make an object or experience different next time (e.g., "What if it rained?").
• Encourage children to recall what they did before the most recent event (e.g., "Help me remember what you did just before you put the dolls to sleep").	• Encourage children to share the sequence of their work-time activities.	• Ask children why they think something will turn out the same way (e.g., "Were you worried your clothes would get wet again?").

Approaches to Learning Strategies: A Summary

General teaching strategies that support approaches to learning

- Establish a physical environment that is rich in options to explore materials, actions, ideas, and relationships.

- Create a daily routine that allows children to express a variety of learning styles and preferences.

- Give children time to approach learning in their own way.

Teaching strategies that support initiative

- Focus on effort, not outcome.

- Acknowledge when children try new things.

- Balance freedom and structure in the physical environment.

- Encourage children's initiative during adult-initiated parts of the day.

Teaching strategies that support planning

- Establish a consistent planning time in the daily routine.

- Provide opportunities for intentional choices throughout the day.

- Show interest in the choices and decisions children make.

Teaching strategies that support engagement

- Provide materials and activities that hold children's interest.

- Give children ample time to carry out their intentions.

- Minimize interruptions and transitions.

Teaching strategies that support problem solving

- Encourage children to describe the problems they encounter.

- Give children time to come up with their own solutions.

- Talk with children about what is and is not working.

- Assist children who are frustrated.

Teaching strategies that support use of resources

- Provide open-ended materials and experiences that appeal to all the senses.

- Talk with children about how they use materials.

- Encourage children to use a variety of resources to answer their own questions.

Teaching strategies that support reflection

- Establish a consistent recall time in the daily routine.

- Make comments and ask questions that encourage reflection.

- Use photographs and mementos to help children remember and reflect on experiences.

References

Alexander, K. L., Entwistle, D. R., & Dauber, S. L. (1993). First-grade classroom behavior: Its short- and long-term consequences for school performance. *Child Development, 64*, 801–815. doi:10.2307/1131219

Bodrova, E., & Leong, D. (2007). *Tools of the mind: The Vygotskian approach to early childhood education* (2nd ed.). New York, NY: Prentice Hall.

Bredekamp, S. (2010). Learning and cognitive development. In V. Washington & J. D. Andrews (Eds.), *Children of 2020: Creating a better tomorrow*. Washington, DC: Council for Professional Recognition.

Catherwood, D. (1999). New views on the young brain: Offerings from developmental psychology to early childhood education. *Contemporary Issues in Early Childhood Education, 1*(1), 23–35.

Chess, S., & Alexander, T. (1996). Temperament. In M. Lewis (Ed.), *Child and adolescent psychiatry: A comprehensive textbook* (2nd ed., pp. 170–181). Baltimore, MD: Williams & Wilkins.

Cooper-Kahn, J., & Dietzel, L. (2008). *Late, lost, and unprepared*. Bethesda, MD: Woodbine House.

Dickinson, D. K., & Smith, M. W. (1994). Long-term effects of preschool teachers' book reading on low-income children's vocabulary and story comprehension. *Reading Research Quarterly, 29*(2), 105–122.

Dowling, J. L., & Mitchell, T. C. (2007). *I belong: Active learning for children with special needs*. Ypsilanti, MI: HighScope Press.

Duncan, G. J., Claessens, A., & Engel, M. (2005, April). The contributions of hard skills and socioemotional behavior to school readiness in ECLS-K. In G. Duncan (Chair), *Hard skills and socioemotional behavior at school entry: What matters most for subsequent achievement?* Symposium conducted at the Biennial Meeting of the Society for Research in Child Development, Atlanta, GA.

Dweck, C. S. (2002). The development of ability conceptions. In A. Wigfield & J. S. Eccles (Eds.), *Development of achievement motivation* (pp. 57–90). San Diego, CA: Academic Press.

Elias, M. J., Zins, J. E., Weissberg, K. S., Frey, M. T., Greenberg, N. M., Kessler, R.,… Shriver, T. P. (1997). *Promoting social and emotional learning: Guidelines for educators*. Alexandria, VA: Association for Supervision and Curriculum Development.

Epstein, A. S. (1993). *Training for quality: Improving early childhood programs through systematic inservice training*. Ypsilanti, MI: HighScope Press.

Epstein, A. S. (2003). How planning and reflection develop young children's thinking skills. *Young Children, 58*(5), 28–36.

Epstein, A. S., & Hohmann, M. (2012). *The HighScope Preschool Curriculm*. Ypsilanti, MI: HighScope Press.

Fantuzzo, J. W., Perry, M. A., & McDermott, P. (2004). Preschool approaches to learning and their relationship to other relevant classroom competencies for low-income children. *School Psychology Quarterly, 19*(3), 212–230. doi:10.1521/scpq.19.3.212.40276

Flavell, J. H., Miller, P. H., & Miller, S. A. (2001). *Cognitive development* (4th ed.). New York, NY: Prentice Hall.

Gardner, H. (1983/2003). *Frames of mind: The theory of multiple intelligences*. New York, NY: Basic Books.

Hyson, M. (2008). *Enthusiastic and engaged learners: Approaches to learning in the early childhood classroom*. New York, NY: Teachers College Press and Washington, DC: National Association for the Education of Young Children.

Kagan, J. (2005). Temperament and the reactions to unfamiliarity. In M. Gauvain & M. Cole. (Eds.), *Readings on the development of children* (4th ed., pp. 73–78). New York, NY: Worth.

Kagan, S. L., Moore, E., & Bredekamp, S. (Eds.). (1995, June). *Reconsidering children's early development and learning: Toward common views and vocabulary* (Goal 1 Technical Planning Group Report 95-03). Washington, DC: National Education Goals Panel.

Katz, L. (1993). *Dispositions, definitions, and implications for early childhood practice*. Champaign, IL: ERIC Clearing House on Elementary and Early Childhood Education.

Katz, L., & McClellan, D. (1997). *Fostering children's social competence: The teacher's role*. Washington, DC: National Association for the Education of Young Children.

Li-Grining, C., Maldonado-Carreño, C., Votruba-Drzal, E., & Haas, K. (2010). Children's early approaches to learning and academic trajectories through fifth grade. *Developmental Psychology, 46*(5), 1062–1077.

Montie, J. E., Xiang, Z., & Schweinhart, L. J. (2006). Preschool experience in 10 countries: Cognitive and language performance at age 7. *Early Childhood Research Quarterly, 21*(3), 313–331. doi:10.1016/j.ecresq.2006.07.007

National Research Council. (2001). *Eager to learn: Educating our preschoolers*. Washington, DC: National Academies Press.

Rothbart, M. K., Sheese, B. E., & Posner, M. (2007). Executive function and effortful control: Linking temperament, brain networks, and genes. *Child Development Perspectives, 1*(1), 2–7.

Shore, R. (2003). *Rethinking the brain: New insights into early development* (Rev. ed.). New York, NY: Families and Work Institute.

Stipek, D. (2002). *Motivation to learn: Integrating theory and practice* (4th ed.). Boston, MA: Allyn & Bacon.

Thompson, R. A. (2002). The roots of school readiness in social and emotional development. *The Kauffman Early Education Exchange, 1,* 8–29.

US Department of Health and Human Services, Administration for Children and Families, Head Start Bureau. (2002, October). *Program Performance Standards and other regulations*. Washington, DC: US Government Printing Office.

Worth, K., & Grollman, S. (2003). *Worms, shadows, and whirlpools: Science in the early childhood classroom*. Portsmouth, NH: Heinemann and Washington, DC: National Association for the Education of Young Children.

Zelazo, P. D., Muller, U., Frye, D., & Marcovitch, S. (2003). The development of executive function. *Monographs of the Society for Research in Child Development, 68*(3), Serial No. 274.